This book is a gift of the
Friends of the Orinda Library

Join us at
friendsoftheorindalibrary.org

PLANET EARTH

the world in infographics

jon richards
and ed simkins

Owl
kids

CONTENTS

WELCOME TO THE WORLD
OF INFOGRAPHICS

Using icons, graphics, and pictograms, infographics visualize data and information in a whole new way!

COMPARE THE TALLEST MOUNTAINS FROM EACH CONTINENT

SEE THE ENTIRE VOLUME OF WATER ON EARTH POURED INTO ONE GLASS

SEE HOW MANY TIMES THE 20 LONGEST RIVERS COULD WRAP AROUND THE EARTH

STACK UP EIFFEL TOWERS TO SEE HOW HIGH THE TALLEST WATERFALL IS

COMPARE THE WORLD'S LONGEST RIVERS

INSIDE THE EARTH

Slicing the entire Earth in half would show that its inside is divided into different layers. These layers push down on each other, creating high pressures and temperatures inside the planet.

CRUST

INNER AND OUTER CORE

MANTLE

0.4%

The crust makes up just 0.4 percent of the Earth's mass, the core makes up about 30 percent, while the mantle makes up nearly 70 percent.

MANTLE 62 MI. (100 KM) TO 1,802 MI. (2,900 KM)

OUTER CORE 1,802 MI. (2,900 KM) TO 3,169 MI. (5,100

ER CORE 1,802 MI. (2,900 KM) TO 3,169 MI. (5,100

3,963 mi. (6,378 km)

The distance from the surface to the center of the Earth is 3,963 mi. (6,378 km), the same distance from London to Chicago.

The temperature inside the Earth increases with **depth**. This is called the **geothermal gradient**.

WARMING UP
The pressures and temperatures inside the Earth are high enough to melt rock.

CRUST UP TO A DEPTH OF 62 MI. (100 KM)

ER CORE 3,169 MI. (5,100 KM) TO 3,963 MI. (6,3...

MOLTEN ROCK IS CONSTANTLY ON THE MOVE

8,852–11,012°F
(4,900–6,100°C)

The inner core is **as hot as** the surface of the **Sun**.

INNER CORE 8,852–11,012°F (4,900–6,100°C)

OUTER CORE 8,132–9,032°F (4,500–5,000°C)

SURFACE **AVERAGE** 59°F (15°C)

ON THE **MOVE**

The Earth's crust is broken up into tectonic plates. As the molten rock of the mantle swirls about under the crust, it pushes and pulls these plates around.

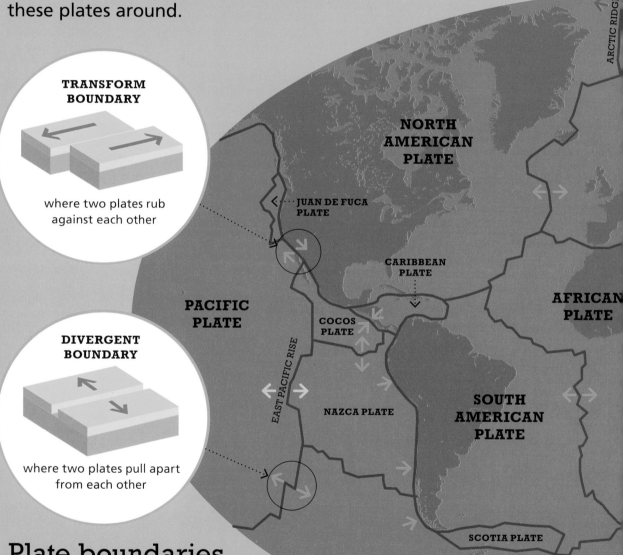

TRANSFORM BOUNDARY

where two plates rub against each other

DIVERGENT BOUNDARY

where two plates pull apart from each other

NORTH AMERICAN PLATE

ARCTIC RIDGE

JUAN DE FUCA PLATE

CARIBBEAN PLATE

PACIFIC PLATE

AFRICAN PLATE

COCOS PLATE

EAST PACIFIC RISE

NAZCA PLATE

SOUTH AMERICAN PLATE

SCOTIA PLATE

ANTARCTIC PLATE

Plate boundaries

The place where two plates meet is called a boundary. Plates rub together, pull apart, or slam into each other. This movement of the crust between two plates can cause volcanic activity and earthquakes.

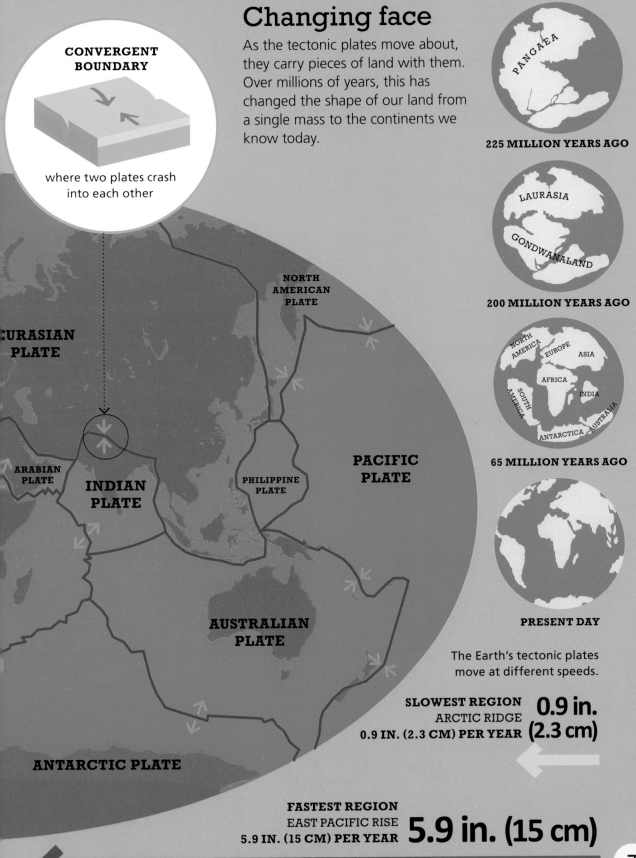

Changing face

As the tectonic plates move about, they carry pieces of land with them. Over millions of years, this has changed the shape of our land from a single mass to the continents we know today.

CONVERGENT BOUNDARY

where two plates crash into each other

PANGAEA

225 MILLION YEARS AGO

LAURASIA

GONDWANALAND

200 MILLION YEARS AGO

NORTH AMERICA
EUROPE
ASIA
AFRICA
INDIA
SOUTH AMERICA
ANTARCTICA
AUSTRALIA

65 MILLION YEARS AGO

PRESENT DAY

NORTH AMERICAN PLATE

EURASIAN PLATE

ARABIAN PLATE

INDIAN PLATE

PHILIPPINE PLATE

PACIFIC PLATE

AUSTRALIAN PLATE

ANTARCTIC PLATE

The Earth's tectonic plates move at different speeds.

SLOWEST REGION
ARCTIC RIDGE
0.9 IN. (2.3 CM) PER YEAR
0.9 in. (2.3 cm)

FASTEST REGION
EAST PACIFIC RISE
5.9 IN. (15 CM) PER YEAR
5.9 in. (15 cm)

RESTLESS EARTH

The Earth's moving tectonic plates sometimes catch against each other and get stuck before releasing suddenly. This sudden release causes earthquakes.

Strong or weak?

The strength of an earthquake is known as its magnitude. This is measured by the Richter scale—the higher the number, the stronger the earthquake. The scale has no upper limit, but an earthquake with a magnitude of 10 or higher has never been recorded.

830,000

Death toll in the deadliest earthquake ever recorded. It occurred in the Shaanxi province of China in 1556.

7.8
1906 SAN FRANCISCO (USA)

8.0
1985 MEXICO CITY (MEXICO)

8.1
1650 CUZCO (PERU)

9.5
1960 VALDIVIA AND PUERTO MONTT (CHILE)

This map (left) highlights where major earthquakes occur. Most earthquakes occur at or near plate boundaries.

8.5

THE TSAR BOMBA WAS DETONATED IN 1961 AND CAUSED THE MOST POWERFUL NUCLEAR EXPLOSION. IT RELEASED THE SAME AMOUNT OF ENERGY AS AN EARTHQUAKE MEASURING 8.5 ON THE RICHTER SCALE.

MOST

Many countries can claim to have had the most earthquakes, including Japan, Indonesia, Fiji, Tonga, China, and Iran.

7.7
1780 TABRIZ (IRAN)

9.0
2011 HONSHU (JAPAN)

9.1
2004 ACEH PROVINCE (INDONESIA)

Of the **500,000** earthquakes that are detected each year (several million actually occur each year), **100,000** can be felt and **100** can cause damage.

FEWEST

Small earthquakes can occur anywhere, but Antarctica is the continent with the fewest earthquakes.

MAGNITUDE	NUMBER
2–2.9	1,300,000
3–3.9	130,000
4–4.9	13,000
5–5.9	1,319
6–6.9	134
7–7.9	15
8.0+	1

NUMBER AND MAGNITUDE OF EARTHQUAKES PER YEAR

Every day, about

55

tons of rock is added to our planet from outer space—more than the weight of ten elephants! These fall to the Earth as meteorites.

1,472–2,372°F (800–1,300°C)

The temperature of magma when it comes to the surface, or erupts, from volcanoes.

LAVA COOLS TO FORM IGNEOUS ROCK

ROCKS SLOWLY PUSHED TO SURFACE

IGNEOUS ROCK

MAGMA COOLS

ROCKS BURIED, SQUEEZED, AND HEATED

MAGMA

ROCKS MELT

METAMORPHIC ROCK

THE ROCK CYCLE

As tectonic plates move about, rock is pushed down into the Earth, where it melts. Other rock is pushed up to the surface, where it is worn away, or eroded, by wind, ice, and water. These changes are part of the rock cycle.

RAIN AND WIND ERODE ROCKS

ROCK PARTICLES TRANSPORTED BY RIVERS

ROCK PARTICLES FALL TO SEA FLOOR

LAYERS OF ROCK SQUEEZED TOGETHER

SEDIMENTARY ROCK

Rock types

There are three types of rock. Igneous rocks are formed from molten rock. Sedimentary rock is formed when tiny pieces of rock settle at the bottom of the sea, where they are compressed. Metamorphic rock is formed when rocks are changed through heat and pressure.

80%

About 80 percent of the rocks at the Earth's surface are sedimentary.

11

VIOLENT
VOLCANOES

Volcanoes form when molten rock travels up from the Earth's mantle and erupts onto the surface. These eruptions can be quick and explosive or long and relatively peaceful.

TYPES OF VOLCANOES

After lava erupts out of a volcano, it cools to form solid rock, creating the cone of the volcano. The shape of the cone depends on the type of lava. For example, runny lava creates a low, wide shield volcano.

SHIELD VOLCANO

COMPOUND/COMPLEX VOLCANO WITH AN OLD CONE

STRATOVOLCANO

CALDERA VOLCANO

YELLOWSTONE
HUCKLEBERRY RIDGE
(2.1 MYA)
588 MI.³ (2,450 KM³

ENOUGH TO FILL
GREAT BEAR LAKE, CANADA

BIGGEST ERUPTIONS

This infographic shows the amount of magma, in cubic miles (mi.3) and cubic kilometers (km3), produced by some of the biggest eruptions, along with their dates (MYA is "millions of years ago"). The eruption at Lake Toba in Indonesia was the largest ever.

ASH CLOUD

In 1991, the eruption of Mount Pinatubo in the Philippines sent an enormous cloud of ash to heights of 21 mi. (34 km). The cloud covered an area of 48,263 mi.² (125,000 km²)— about half the size of the state of Mississippi.

THE EXPLOSION OF KRAKATOA IN INDONESIA IN 1883 HAD A FORCE EQUIVALENT TO

10,000

ATOMIC BOMBS.

FORMING A CORAL ATOLL

1. Volcanic cone forms above sea level.

2. When volcano stops erupting, a ring of coral, called an atoll, forms around the cone.

3. Coral continues to grow while volcano cone is eroded.

4. Volcano cone erodes below sea level, leaving atoll above water.

YELLOWSTONE MESA FALLS
(1.3 MYA)
67 MI.³
(280 KM³)

LONG VALLEY CALDERA
(760,000 YA)
144 MI.³ (600 KM³)

YELLOWSTONE LAVA CREEK
(640,000 YA)
240 MI.³ (1,000 KM³)

TOBA
(74,000 YA)
672 MI.³ (2,800 KM³)

ENOUGH TO FILL LAKE VICTORIA, AFRICA

TOWERING
PEAKS

When tectonic plates crash into each other, they can push the ground up to form mountains. Mountains are often grouped together in long chains near plate boundaries.

■ MOUNTAIN RANGES

←·············· The tallest mountain in the world is part of the Himalayan mountain range.

This is the tallest peak in the Andes, which run the length of South America.

EVEREST
ASIA
29,029 ft.
(8,848 m)

ACONCAGUA
SOUTH AMERICA
22,841 ft.
(6,962 m)

ELBRUS
EUROPE
18,511 ft.
(5,642 m)

The tallest peak in Europe is a volcano that is part of the Caucasus range, which lies in Russia near the border with Georgia.

Changes

Climate and conditions change as you climb a mountain, affecting the kinds of plants and animals that can live at different heights. Places that are higher up a mountain will be colder and may well be wetter than those lower down. Anything living here will have to adapt to these conditions.

ALPINE ZONE ←······· SNOW LINE

TREE LINE ······→

SUBALPINE ZONE
UP TO 13,025 ft. (3,970 m)

TEMPERATE ZONE
UP TO 8,005 ft. (2,440 m)

SUBTROPICAL ZONE
UP TO 6,004 ft. (1,830 m)

9,942 mi. (16,000 km)

The world's longest mountain range is the Mid-Atlantic Ridge. It runs along the entire length of the Atlantic Ocean and is completely submerged.

The tallest peak in North America was formed by a collision between the Pacific and North American plates.

Kilimanjaro is the highest peak in Africa and is not part of a mountain chain.

McKINLEY (DENALI)
NORTH AMERICA
20,322 ft. (6,194 m)

KILIMANJARO
AFRICA
19,341 ft. (5,895 m)

VINSON MASSIF
ANTARCTICA
16,066 ft. (4,897 m)

Part of the Ellsworth Mountains, this peak is just 746 mi. (1,200 km) from the South Pole.

CARSTENSZ PYRAMID
OCEANIA

Located on New Guinea, this mountain was formed by a collision between the Australian and Pacific plates.

16,024 ft. (4,884 m)

15

HABITATS

From teeming coral reefs to densely packed forests, the world is covered in a wide range of habitats. The type of habitat is determined by what the climatic conditions are in a region.

POLAR AND TUNDRA

TEMPERATE FOREST

SAVANNAH

TROPICAL FOREST

MOUNTAIN VEGETATION

29%
OF EARTH
IS LAND

71%
OF EARTH
IS AQUATIC,
OF WHICH:

1% IS COVERED BY CORAL REEFS

2.5% IS FRESHWATER

29%
OF EARTH IS LAND, OF WHICH:

31% DESERT
INCLUDING THE POLES

33% GRASSLAND
INCLUDING TEMPERATE GRASSLAND AND SAVANNAH

36% FOREST
INCLUDING TROPICAL AND CONIFEROUS FOREST (TAIGA)

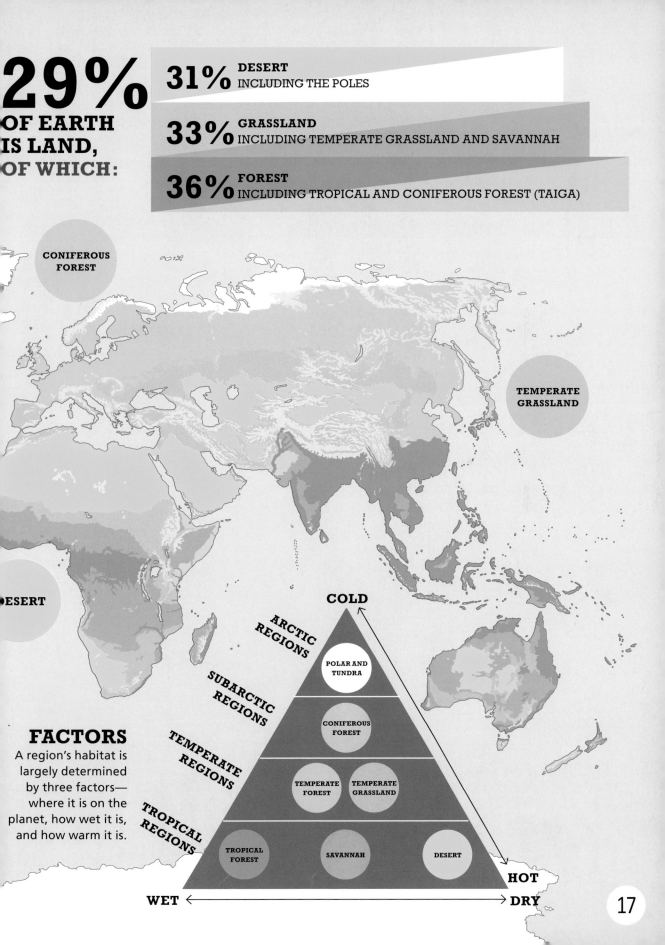

CONIFEROUS FOREST

TEMPERATE GRASSLAND

DESERT

FACTORS

A region's habitat is largely determined by three factors—where it is on the planet, how wet it is, and how warm it is.

COLD

ARCTIC REGIONS

SUBARCTIC REGIONS

TEMPERATE REGIONS

TROPICAL REGIONS

POLAR AND TUNDRA

CONIFEROUS FOREST

TEMPERATE FOREST

TEMPERATE GRASSLAND

TROPICAL FOREST

SAVANNAH

DESERT

HOT

WET ← → DRY

THE AIR WE BREATHE

Surrounding our planet is a thin layer of gases called the atmosphere. It contains the air that is vital for us to live, and it produces all of our weather. The atmosphere is made up of many layers.

THERMOSPHERE
53–398 MI. (85–640 KM)

MESOSPHERE
31–53 MI. (50–85 KM)

SPACESHIPONE
FIRST MANNED PRIVATE SPACEFLIGHT
70 MI. (112 KM)

STRATO-LAB V
HIGHEST MANNED BALLOON
21 MI. (34 KM) ····>

STRATOSPHERE
11–31 MI. (18–50 KM)

MODERN PASSENGER JET
CRUISING ALTITUDE 6 MI. (10 KM)

CIRRUS

CIRROSTRATUS

ALTOCUMULUS

NIMBOSTRATUS

CUMULONIMBUS

STRATUS   CUMULUS

TROPOSPHERE
**WITH CLOUDS UP TO
11 MI. (18 KM)
FROM THE SURFACE**

WIND SPEED

As air is heated by the Sun, it starts to move around, creating wind. Wind speed is measured using the Beaufort scale. A measure of 1 is almost still, while 12 will blow down buildings.

1 2 3 4 5 6

7 8 9 10 11 12

HUBBLE SPACE TELESCOPE
347 MI. (559 KM)

EXOSPHERE
ABOVE 398 MI. (640 KM)

INTERNATIONAL SPACE STATION (ISS)
173–286 MI. (278–460 KM)

254 mph (408 km/h)

The fastest wind speed ever recorded. It was measured at an automatic weather station on Barrow Island, Australia, during Tropical Cyclone Olivia on April 10, 1996.

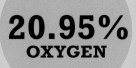

78.08%
NITROGEN

20.95%
OXYGEN

0–4%
WATER VAPOR

0.93%
ARGON

0.038%
CARBON DIOXIDE

What's in air?

Most of the air we breathe in is made up of the gas nitrogen. About one-fifth of air is made up of oxygen, which is the gas we need to stay alive. There are also tiny amounts of other gases, including argon and carbon dioxide.

WATER CYCLE

Water is vital for life. It also plays an important part in the weather and in shaping the land. Water moves around our planet in a system called the water cycle.

1,102,000,000,000

EACH DAY, THE SUN CAUSES MORE THAN ONE TRILLION TONS OF WATER TO EVAPORATE.

CONDENSATION

80%
OF THE EARTH'S WATER IS SURFACE WATER.

THE REMAINING **20%** IS EITHER GROUNDWATER OR ATMOSPHERIC WATER VAPOR.

EVAPORATION
FROM OCEANS AND LAKES

TRANSPIRATION
FROM PLANTS

121,156 MI.³
(505,000 KM³)

The volume of water that falls as precipitation each year all around the Earth.

PRECIPITATION

SNOW MELT

104,122 MI.³
(434,000 KM³)

The amount of water that evaporates from the Earth's oceans in a year.

Nearly **all** of the water found in the atmosphere lies within the **troposphere**, the part of the atmosphere up to **11 mi. (18 km)** above the surface.

SURFACE RUNOFF

GROUNDWATER

OCEANS AND LAKES

3%

The average amount of salt and minerals found in seawater.

WATER **WORLD**

Water covers 71 percent of the Earth's surface, in seas, oceans, and rivers. But water is also found in the air we breathe and frozen in the ice caps near the poles. Just how much water is there on our planet?

0.3 BILLION MI.^{3}
(1.4 BILLION KM^3)

The total volume of all the water on our planet and in the atmosphere.

EARTH'S DIAMETER 7,926 MI. (12,756 KM)

IF THE WORLD'S WATER WERE MADE INTO A BALL, IT WOULD MEASURE 864 MI. (1,390 KM) ACROSS.

ICEBERG B15 183 MI. (295 KM) LONG

The world's largest iceberg, called B15, broke away from Antarctica in 2000. Parts of it still haven't melted.

JAMAICA 145 MI. (234 KM) LONG

MASS OF ICEBERG B15 WAS MORE THAN THREE BILLION TONS **3,306,000,000**

FRESHWATER
2.5%

OF THE
FRESHWATER:

GLACIERS
68.7%

SALTWATER IN
OCEANS, SEAS,
GROUNDWATER,
AND LAKES
97.5%

GROUNDWATER
30.1%

PERMANENTLY FROZEN IN THE
GROUND (PERMAFROST) 0.8%

WATER IN THE AIR AND ON THE
EARTH'S SURFACE 0.4%

RAINFALL RECORDS

Most in one minute: 1.2 in. (31.2 mm); Unionville, Maryland, USA, July 4, 1956

Most in 60 minutes: 12 in. (305 mm) in 42 minutes; Holt, Missouri, USA, June 22, 1947

Most in 12 hours: 45 in. (1,144 mm); Foc-Foc, Réunion, January 8, 1966, during Tropical Cyclone Denis

Most in 24 hours: 72 in. (1,825 mm); Foc-Foc, Réunion, January 7–8, 1966

Most in 48 hours: 97 in. (2,467 mm); Aurère, Réunion, January 8–10, 1958

Most in 72 hours: 155 in. (3,929 mm); Commerson, Réunion, February 24–26, 2007

Most in 96 hours: 192 in. (4,869 mm); Commerson, Réunion, February 24–27, 2007

Most in one year: 1,042 in. (26,470 mm); Cherrapunji, India, 1860–1861

Highest average annual total: 467 in. (11,872 mm); Mawsynram, India

SCUBA DIVING 1,083 FT. ······> (330 M)

<······ FREE DIVING 702 FT. (214 M)

<······ ATMOSPHERIC DIVING SUIT 2,001 FT. (610 M)

3,281 FT. (1,000 M)

<······ MILITARY SUBMARINE 4,265 FT. (1,300 M)

SPERM WHALE 9,843 FT. (3,000 M)

ANGLERFISH 9,843 FT. (3,000 M)

<······ COLOSSAL SQUID 7,218 FT. (2,200 M)

WRECK OF *TITANIC* ······> 12,402 FT. (3,780 M)

13,124 FT. (4,000 M)

APHOTIC ZONE

THE OCEANS

Beneath the surface of the Earth's seas and oceans is a varied world of different regions that reach down to the darkest depths.

CUSK-EEL 27,461 FT. (8,370 M)

26,247 FT. (8,000 M)

Under pressure

The oceans are divided into different zones. The photic zone is the part of the ocean where sunlight can reach. Beneath it is the dark aphotic zone. Pressures become greater as depths increase. Just 33 ft. (10 m) below the waves, the pressure is already twice that at the surface.

THE SUBMERSIBLE *TRIESTE* HOLDS THE RECORD FOR THE DEEPEST DIVE EVER MADE— 35,797 FT. (10,911 M) BELOW THE SURFACE.

TRIESTE

35,797 FT. (10,911 M)

46.5%

The percentage of the world's oceans made up by the Pacific—almost as much as the Indian, Atlantic, Southern, and Arctic oceans put together.

- 6% SOUTHERN OCEAN
- 4.1% ARCTIC OCEAN
- 20.5% INDIAN OCEAN
- 22.9% ATLANTIC OCEAN
- 46.5% PACIFIC OCEAN

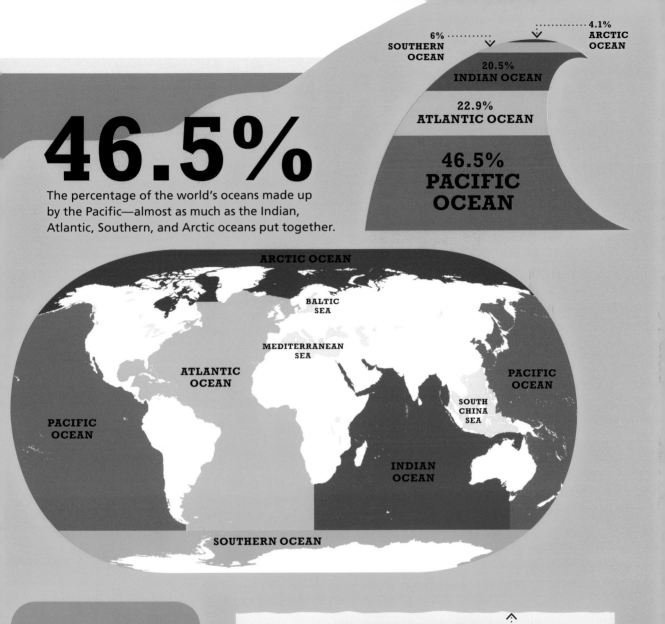

ARCTIC OCEAN

BALTIC SEA

MEDITERRANEAN SEA

ATLANTIC OCEAN

PACIFIC OCEAN

PACIFIC OCEAN

SOUTH CHINA SEA

INDIAN OCEAN

SOUTHERN OCEAN

If all the **salt** were taken out of the oceans, it would cover the land to a depth of

5 ft. (1.5 m).

The deepest part of the ocean is deeper than the highest peak on the Earth.

CHALLENGER DEEP
36,204 FT. (11,035 M) BELOW SEA LEVEL

MOUNT EVEREST
29,029 FT. (8,848 M) HIGH

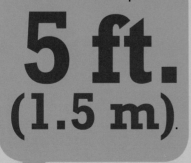

RAGING **RIVERS**

Some of the Earth's rivers are so large that they stretch for thousands of miles. They tumble over towering waterfalls and meander through the countryside, carrying enormous amounts of water across the land.

rivers	source	countries crossed
NILE	LAKE VICTORIA	ETHIOPIA **SUDAN** SOUTH SUDAN **EGYPT** UGANDA **TANZANIA** RWANDA **DEMOCRATIC REPUBLIC OF THE CONGO** KENYA **BURUNDI** ERITREA
AMAZON-UCAYALI-APURÍMAC	ANDES MOUNTAINS	BRAZIL **COLOMBIA** ECUADOR **PERU**
YANGTZE	TANGGULA MOUNTAINS	CHINA
MISSISSIPPI-MISSOURI-RED ROCK	LAKE ITASCA	UNITED STATES
YENISEI-BAIKAL-SELENGA	MUNGARAGIYN-GOL	MONGOLIA **RUSSIA**
HUANG HE (YELLOW)	BAYAN HAR MOUNTAINS	CHINA
OB-IRTYSH	BELUKHA MOUNTAIN	RUSSIA
PARANÁ	RIO PARANAÍBA	ARGENTINA **BRAZIL** PARAGUAY
rivers	source	countries crossed

> The world's **20** largest rivers **discharge** enough water to fill a **football stadium** in **3** seconds.

River discharge

The amount of water that a river releases into a sea or lake is called its discharge. A river's discharge depends on the local climate and the size of its drainage basin, which is the area of land that the river empties of water.

RIVERS WITH THE GREATEST DISCHARGE
cubic feet per second (ft.³/s)
cubic meters per second (m³/s)

RIO NEGRO	MADEIRA	ORINOCO	YANGTZE
1,003,000 ft.³/s (28,400 m³/s)	1,102,000 ft.³/s (31,200 m³/s)	1,165,000 ft.³/s (33,000 m³/s)	1,236,000 ft.³/s (35,000 m³/s)

250,000

The number of rivers there are in the United States, with a combined total length of more than 3.5 million miles (5.6 million kilometers).

If you put the 20 longest rivers end to end, they would wrap around the equator more than

twice.

ends	length
MEDITERRANEAN SEA	**4,132 mi. (6,650 km)**
ATLANTIC OCEAN	**3,977 mi. (6,400 km)**
EAST CHINA SEA	**3,915 mi. (6,300 km)**
GULF OF MEXICO	**3,710 mi. (5,971 km)**
YENISEI GULF	**3,442 mi. (5,540 km)**
BOHAI SEA	**3,396 mi. (5,465 km)**
GULF OF OB	**3,362 mi. (5,410 km)**
RIO DE LA PLATA	**3,032 mi. (4,880 km)**

ends .... length

CONGO
1,455,000 ft.³/s
(41,200 m³/s)

AMAZON
6,180,000 ft.³/s
(175,000 m³/s)

GANGES
1,500,000 ft.³/s
(42,470 m³/s)

Angel Falls, Venezuela
3,212 ft. (979 m)

3 Eiffel Towers

HIGHEST
WATERFALL
IN THE WORLD

CHANGING EARTH

Conditions on our planet are not fixed. During the Earth's history there have been long periods of the planet heating up and then cooling down. Scientists have discovered that at present, the Earth is getting warmer.

REFLECTED

Some of the Sun's radiation is reflected back out into space by the Earth's surface.

LOST HEAT

When the Earth absorbs the Sun's radiation, it then produces its own radiation as infrared heat. Some of this heat is lost into space.

Rising seas

Increasing temperatures around the world could melt the ice caps at the poles. As a result, sea levels would rise. The red areas on the graphic above are those that would be flooded by a rise in sea levels of 328 ft. (100 m).

AEROSOLS

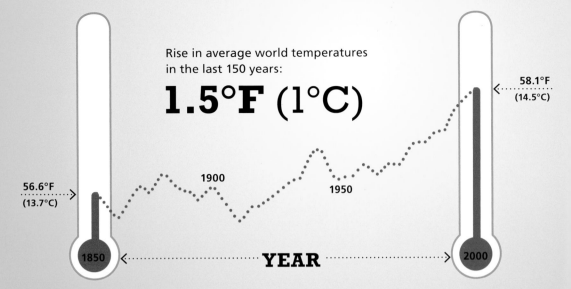

Rise in average world temperatures
in the last 150 years:

1.5°F (1°C)

58.1°F
(14.5°C)

56.6°F
(13.7°C)

1900

1950

1850

YEAR

2000

Warming

Our planet is kept warm by a process called the
greenhouse effect. Gases and other substances
in the atmosphere, such as aerosols, trap the heat
that is reflected or given off by the Earth.

SUN'S RAYS

Nearly three-quarters
of the Sun's radiation
that reaches the
Earth makes it to
the surface.

AEROSOLS

LOST IN SPACE

Some of the Sun's radiation
is reflected straight back
out into space.

GREENHOUSE

Gases and other substances in
the atmosphere trap heat given
off by the Earth, warming up the
atmosphere even more and
creating the greenhouse effect.

GLOSSARY

  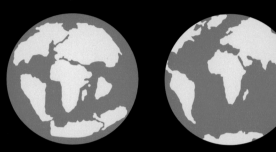

Atoll

A coral reef that goes all or part of the way around an island.

Continents

Large areas of land. The Earth has seven continents: Asia, Africa, North America, South America, Europe, Australia, and Antarctica.

Core

The mass that lies at the center of the Earth. It is divided up into the outer core, which is 1,367 mi. (2,200 km) thick, and an inner core, which has a radius of about 808 mi. (1,300 km).

Igneous

A type of rock that forms from the cooling of magma or lava.

Crust

The outermost layer of the Earth. The Earth's crust is up to 62 mi. (100 km) thick.

Lava

When magma reaches the Earth's surface during a volcanic eruption, it is called lava.

Drainage basin

An area of land that a river drains of water. Rain that falls within this area will flow over or under the ground, collecting together to form streams. These streams will then join together to form the larger river.

Greenhouse effect

The process by which the atmosphere traps heat given off by the Earth before it can escape into space. This trapped heat warms up the atmosphere.

Magma

Molten rock that is found beneath the Earth's surface.

Magnitude

How strong something is. For example, the magnitude of an earthquake is measured by the Richter scale—a higher reading on this scale indicates a stronger earthquake.

Mantle

The region inside the Earth that lies beneath the crust and above the core. It reaches down to a depth of 1,802 mi. (2,900 km) below the surface and is made up of hot molten rock.

Metamorphic
A type of rock that has been created under extreme heat and pressure.

Molten
A substance that has become liquid by getting very hot. For example, the metal iron becomes molten at 2,800°F (1,538°C).

Pangaea
The name given to the enormous piece of land formed on the Earth 270 million years ago.

Precipitation
Water that falls to the ground as rain or snow.

Radiation
A type of energy that is released in wave form, such as light, or as tiny subatomic particles.

Richter scale
The scale used to measure the strength of an earthquake—the higher the number, the more powerful the tremor.

Sedimentary
A type of rock that is formed by small rock particles that have settled in water and been squashed together.

Subalpine zone
A region that lies just below the tree line on the side of a mountain.

Subarctic zone
The region that lies between the Arctic and the temperate regions.

Taiga
A type of coniferous forest that is found in a large band south of the Arctic, running through North America, northern Europe, and Russia.

Tectonic plates
The large pieces of the Earth's surface that fit together to form the crust. These pieces crash into each other, pull apart, or rub against one another.

Transpiration
When plants give off water vapor.

Resources

MORE INFO:

www.noaa.gov
Home page of the National Oceanic and Atmospheric Administration, including an education section for teachers and students.

www.usgs.gov
The US Geological Survey studies the state of the world's habitats and the environment, as well as natural hazards such as earthquakes.

MORE GRAPHICS:
www.visualinformation.info
A website that contains a whole host of infographic material on subjects as diverse as natural history, science, sports, and computer games.

www.coolinfographics.com
A collection of infographics and data visualizations from other online resources, magazines, and newspapers.

www.dailyinfographic.com
A comprehensive collection of infographics on an enormous range of topics that is updated every single day!

The following sources were consulted to create this book:
United States Geological Survey; *Encyclopedia Britannica*; BBC Online; and the *Independent* newspaper.

INDEX

Owlkids Books Inc.
10 Lower Spadina Avenue, Suite 400,
Toronto, Ontario M5V 2Z2
www.owlkidsbooks.com

Published in North America in 2013
© 2012 Wayland

Distributed in Canada by
University of Toronto Press
5201 Dufferin Street, Toronto, Ontario
M3H 5T8

Distributed in the United States by
Publishers Group West
1700 Fourth Street, Berkeley, California
94710

Library and Archives Canada Cataloguing in Publication

Richards, Jon, 1970-
    Planet earth / written by Jon Richards ; illustrated by
Ed Simkins.

(The world in infographics)
Includes index.
ISBN 978-1-926973-75-3

    1. Physical geography--Juvenile literature. 2. Earth--
Juvenile literature. I. Simkins, Ed II. Title. III. Series:
World in infographics

GB58.R52 2013   j910'.02   C2012-905422-4

Library of Congress Control Number: 2012951085

We acknowledge the financial support of the Canada Council for the
Arts, the Ontario Arts Council, the Government of Canada through
the Canada Book Fund (CBF) and the Government of Ontario through
the Ontario Media Development Corporation's Book Initiative for our
publishing activities.

Manufactured by WKT Co. Ltd.
Manufactured in Shenzhen, Guangdong, China, in November 2012
Job #12CB1352

A   B   C   D   E

Publisher of Chirp, chickaDEE and OW
www.owlkidsbooks.com

Canadian Heritage / Patrimoine canadien

Canada Council for the Arts / Conseil des Arts du Canada

ONTARIO ARTS COUNCIL / CONSEIL DES ARTS DE L'ONTARIO

Ontario / Ontario Media Development Corporation / Société de développement de l'industrie des médias de l'Ontario